Tao

The cover illustration by Jane Evans is an adaptation from actual Chinese watercolors in "A History of Far Eastern Art" by Sherman E. Lee. Lao-Tsze frequently used water as a symbol in his teachings.

Goodness and water are the same
In that each often runs
Through lowly spots, unknown to fame,
Which the self-seeker shuns.

Tao

A poetic version of the Tao Teh Ching
of Lao Tsze

Translated by **Charles A. Mackintosh**

This publication made possible with the
assistance of the Kern Foundation.

The Theosophical Publishing House
Wheaton, Ill. / Madras, India / London, England

Fourth Quest printing, 1986. Published by the
Theosophical Publishing House, a department of
the Theosophical Society in America.

ISBN: 0-8356-0426-8

Printed in the United States of America

FOREWORD

CONCISENESS is the keynote to this work. The ancient original manuscript contained only 5,000 characters, which have been incredibly expanded in translation into English. Some expansion is, of course, essential, since an ideograph is an idea and not simply one word; but an idea dissolved in too many words is weakened thereby like a drug dissolved in too much water. And so the task of this translation has been to retain the rhythmical motif which is so often apparent in the original without sacrificing the crystalline conciseness of its epigrammatic style. There are approximately 6,500 English words in this version. The original manuscript was not divided into sections, or chapters, by its author, nor does it lend itself to such division since the flow of thought frequently changes its course with considerable abruptness. In this version it has been deemed best, in accord with the purpose of presenting the original atmosphere of the ancient work, to eliminate all subsequent editorial additions in the form of arbitrary divisions and chapter headings, and to present the work as one unbroken whole, even as it came from the hand of the original author.

The author of the original monograph, Li Er, Poh-Yang, known to posterity simply as LAO TSZE (TSZU), "The Venerable Philosopher," is said to have been born six hundred and four years before Christ, and to have been keeper of the royal library at the court of Chow in the province of Ho-nan, China.

In extreme old age, he left the court to retire into seclusion, pausing on the way to put into ideographs the brief monograph which has been for twenty-four centuries the accepted authority on Chinese theology, other great philosophers of China — Confucius as the leading example — having largely avoided the theological in favor of the rules of propriety.

TAO is translated by some to mean "The Way"; by others "The Truth" or "Eternal Reason"; others compare it to the Logos or "Word of Life" of the New Testament. Having in mind that passage from the Scriptures with which his Occidental readers are most familiar, in which the Christ states definitely that the Way, the Truth, and the Life are One, the author has not hesitated to use GOD as the most inclusive translation of the original ideograph.

The second word in the original title, TEH, means Virtue, but was used apparently to expand the meaning of the preceding ideograph in order to make it more inclusive. Instead of rendering the two as Reason-Virtue, or as The Word, or Way, of Virtue, the author has followed the example of the Taoists themselves, in concentrating upon the superior thought in a single word.

The word CHING (often written King, although some of the greatest living Chinese educators have assured the author that "Ching" more nearly approximates the Chinese pronunciation) was not part of the original title, but was added centuries later to signify that the work had received Imperial sanction as one of the great classics of China.

The teachings of LAO TSZE compare closely with those of the Christ. He taught that human virtue consists in applying the will of God to all human enterprise, claiming no credit for suc-

cess, since it is simply the will of God that succeeds.

He stresses the virtue of non-assertion, of
doing without demanding recognition, in line
after line of his monograph. The key-thought
is *to do good just as God does — because it is
the natural and inevitable expression of Himself*
— and that is the aim of all true followers of
the Venerable Philosopher.

C. H. M.

T·A·O
The TAO TEH CHING of LAO TSZE
Rendered into English Verse

1

The way to which mankind may hold
    Is not the eternal way.
Eternal truths cannot be told
    In what men write or say.

2

The name that may be named by man
    Is not the eternal name
That was before the world began
    Or human language came.

3

In that the namable took root,
    The tree of fire and force,
Which, having blossomed and borne fruit,
    Returns then to its source.

4

Who warms his body at that fire,
    Sees nothing but its smoke;
But he who puts aside desire,
    The flame's self may invoke.

5

These two things are the same in source
    But different in name;
Who solves this mystery has recourse
    To that from whence he came.

6

Beauty, delighting in display,
    Becomes sheer ugliness;
And so it is that goodness may
    Seem greater, but be less.

7

The holy man prepares the plot
    But does not claim the yield,
He quickens, but possesses not,
    Acts, but remains concealed.

8

He merits much, but does not ask
　　That any grant that same;
He finds his pleasure in the task,
　　And fears to find it fame.

9

Not ever boasting of his worth,
　　No one desires to dim;
Not prizing treasures of the earth,
　　No one will steal from him.

10

All thoughts that kindle to desire,
　　His mind has long refused,
And, since he does not feed that fire,
　　His heart is unconfused.

11

When such a one governs the land,
　　Self-seeking finds surcease.
The crafty dare not raise a hand;
　　The people dwell in peace.

12

God is quite empty, but profound:
    The father, and the seed;
The radiant sky; the dusty ground;
    The doer, and the deed.

13

How calm He is, how calm and still!
    I know not whence He came;
He was before the word of will
    That gave the Lord his name.

14

Were heaven troubled with desire,
    Would it be long before
The worlds were cast into the fire
    Like temple dogs of straw?

15

And if the holy man refused
    To toil save for a price,
Would not his heart become confused,
    Corrupting his advice?

16

Standing upon the mountain steep
    How low the valley seems!
And yet, because it lies so deep,
    It gathers all the streams.

17

The valley-spirit cannot fall
    Because it lies so low;
And yet it is the base of all,
    And to it all things flow.

18

Earth's bulk, and heaven's awful curve,
    How can they so endure?
Neither has selfish ends to serve,
    And so their strength is pure.

19

So it is with the holy one
    Who keeps his spirit meek;
All things that he desires are done,
    Who serves but does not seek.

20

Goodness and water are the same
    In that each often runs
Through lowly spots, unknown to fame,
    Which the self-seeker shuns.

21

Goodness, when great, is lowly still;
    It makes commotion cease;
In giving, goodness shows good will;
    In government, brings peace;

22

In business, brings ability;
    In perfect time it moves;
Going in all humility,
    Therefore no one reproves.

23

Who grasps too much is likely foiled;
    Who schemes too hot, grows cold;
That hall is certain to be spoiled
    Which brims with gems and gold.

24

The rich and high who have the flaw
    Of pride, invite decay.
To do the deed and then withdraw —
    That is the Godlike way.

25

Who knows himself as One, no less,
    Cannot be torn apart;
Who concentrates his tenderness,
    May purify his heart.

26

Who loves the people he would lead,
    Will not proclaim his power,
But act, and quicken them, and feed
    As heaven feeds the flower.

27

The thirty spokes within the wheel
    Unite upon — a hole;
Yet, but for that which none can feel,
    How could the carriage roll?

28

From damp clay molded into place,
    A vessel may be wrought;
And yet, but for its empty space,
    Its value would be naught.

29

Tho' wood and tile may build a hall
    And roof it with a dome,
It is the space within the wall,
    That makes the hall a home.

30

And so, from vessel, hall, and wheel,
    This truth we may deduce:
To what existence renders real,
    Its opposite gives use.

31

If all the colors are combined,
    All notes together sound,
Such light the human eye will blind,
    Such noise the ear confound.

32

When all the tastes together blend,
    The taste is wholly bad.
All sensual pleasures have an end,
    Excess but drives men mad.

33

Who would be wise in word and deed,
    And free from sensual strife,
Permits each sense to serve his need,
    But not to rule his life.

34

Who seeks for favor, fears to fail;
    Who gains it, fears disgrace:
How like the body, quick to ail,
    Is lofty rank and place!

35

Who sits upon the Peacock Throne,
    Keeping his person pure,
And rules the empire as his own
    Body, shall be secure.

36

How colorless is God, and clear,
    Our eyes see nothing real;
We listen, but we do not hear;
    We grasp, but do not feel.

37

We cannot analyze this thought —
    These mysteries that blend;
In the beginning there was naught,
    And shall be at the end.

38

Beginning's self did not begin;
    No ending can there be.
Who holds fast to these truths shall win
    To immortality.

39

The ancient masters, those of yore,
    Were subtle and profound.
How few can understand their lore,
    Which I strive to expound!

40

How cautious they! Like men who cross
    Thin ice to reach firm land.
How hesitant! As fearing loss
    From foes on every hand.

41

And how reserved! Like gentle guests.
    And how elusive they!
Like snow that falls on Summer's breasts,
    And swiftly melts away.

42

How simple! Like the unhewn wood.
    How empty! Like the vale.
And how obscure! The troubled flood,
    Compared, seems clear and pale.

43

But who can quiet the troubled streams?
    And who can stir the stilled?
Who follows on where wisdom gleams
    Cares nothing to be filled.

44

Devoid of worry, fear, and doubt —
    Traps set for foolish feet;
He is not filled, and so, without
    Renewal, grows complete.

45

Who seeks the rest of perfect peace,
    Must know the nameless name,
Whence all things rise, and bloom, and
                       cease,
    Returning whence they came.

46

According thus with destiny,
    The eternal light grows strong.
Without that light, one can but be
    Forever in the wrong.

47

He shall no longer fear decay,
    Who holds this wisdom sure;
For, though his body pass away,
    Himself shall still endure.

48

The subjects of the truly wise
    Perceive no government,
But live as though from cloudless skies
    Rained order and content.

49

The lesser rulers are held dear,
    Their subjects call them wise;
Still lesser ones, the people fear;
    And lesser still, despise.

50

So tenderly those great ones wrought
    The service of the throne;
The hundred families each thought
    "We rule ourselves alone."

51

When the great wisdom is denied,
    Justice must take its place.
When justice in its turn has died,
    Prudence must meet the case.

52

When family chords fall out of tune,
    Then filial piety comes.
Loyalty and allegiance soon
    Follow the warlike drums.

53

Abandon all your saintliness;
    Your prudence put aside;
Then you may rule and truly bless
    And serve the countryside!

54

Go, set aside your justice stern,
    And your benevolence,
So that the people may return
    To simple commonsense!

55

Abandon smartness, give up greed;
    All thought of self resist;
So all shall have all that they need,
    And thieves no more exist!

56

Hold fast to that which shall endure;
    Let your desires be few;
Show yourself simple, and be pure;
    And all shall flow to you!

57

Abandon learning, and your mind
    Will not be vexed by doubt.
Though tight the net of words may bind,
    How surely Truth slips out!

58

To seek all good, all evil spurn,
    Love peace, and flee from strife:
Is that not all the wisest learn,
    And not from books — from life?

59

The multitudes of men are gay,
    Oh, harken how they sing,
As though upon a festal day
    To welcome back the spring.

60

The holy man alone is sad;
    As, by the temple wall,
One fears to find the omen bad,
    Or not received at all.

61

Ah, he is like a little child,
    A moment after birth,
Who has not ever wept or smiled
    Nor recognized the earth.

62

Forlorn is he, forlorn indeed,
    And utterly alone.
Others have plenty for their need,
    Naught has he for his own.

63

While common folk are bright, so bright,
    How ignorant he seems!
When others' wit glows keen and light,
    How dull his wisdom gleams!

64

Desolate, like the empty sea;
    Adrift, no place to moor;
All others have utility,
    He rustic, and a boor!

65

How far he differs from the rest,
    This child of time and chance,
Who lies upon the mother's breast,
    To seek his sustenance!

66

Great virtue is the shade of God;
    God, whom all thought eludes;
Yet all that lives upon the sod
    That deep, obscure, includes.

67

In Him abides the spirit pure
    Whose faith shall never fall;
Eternally He shall endure,
    Heeding the good of all.

68

They that are crooked shall be straight;
    The empty find their fill;
The crushed ones shall recuperate;
    The worn with strength re-thrill.

69

They that have little shall receive,
    And they whose wealth is great,
Shall lose their surplus to relieve
    The more unfortunate.

70

He who embraces unity,
    All men should imitate;
Not self-displaying, he may be
    Enlightened, free, and great.

71

Not self-approving, who is more
    Approved than such as he?
Who does not seek to go before,
    Leader of all shall be.

72

Disdaining disputatious talk,
　　None leads him into strife.
This is the path that all must walk,
　　To lead the perfect life.

73

Great violence cannot last for long;
　　The cloudburst and the gale,
Tho' heaven and earth have made them
　　　　　　　　　　　　strong,
　　How shortly must they fail!

74

If heaven and earth cannot sustain
　　Their violence for a day;
How foolish is that man, and vain,
　　Who gives his passions play!

75

Those who accomplish each affair
　　In God's all-gentle guise,
Shall find companions everywhere
　　As virtuous and wise.

76

From whom good fortune seems to flee
    In work as well as play,
On every side, others shall see
    Unfortunate as they!

77

The virtuous seek the virtuous out;
    The grieving, them that grieve;
And he whose faith is lost in doubt,
    No faith shall he receive.

78

He who displays his wit to all,
    Displays himself a fool;
Asserting self invites a fall,
    And gets it, as a rule.

79

On self-approval, plainly seen
    By others, anger thrives;
Who yields to it, is counted mean;
    Self-seekers stunt their lives.

80

Like one whose bloated body shows
    He loves his food too much;
Or one upon whose person grows
    The wen that none will touch,

81

Self-seeking fools are shunned and left
    Alone by all mankind.
Not so the holy one, bereft
    Of self in heart and mind.

82

Before the earth in space was spun
    Beneath the heaven's feet,
There was a mighty spirit, One,
    Calm, wondrous and complete.

83

Changeless, yet moving; from its womb
    All things came into birth;
This is the mystic bride and groom,
    Maker of heaven and earth.

84

Its name I know not, and none knows.
    Its nature, God, I call;
From whence all came, to which all goes —
    The heart and home of all.

85

Man's simple standard is the earth;
    Earth's standard, Heaven's throne;
Heaven's standard, God who gave it birth;
    God's standard is His own.

86

Rest conquers motion; at the heart
    Of lightness there is mass.
And so the wise one sits apart
    As pleasures come and pass.

87

How is it when the earthly lord
    Delights in joy alone?
Shall he not perish by the sword,
    Or, surely, lose his throne?

88

The skillful traveler leaves no trail
　　To draw foes on his track;
Good speakers' logic does not fail;
　　Good reckoners need no rack.

89

Good treasurers need not bolt nor bar
　　To keep their treasures sound;
Though all may know just where they are,
　　By none may they be found.

90

The holy and enlightened mind
　　That knows all things have worth,
And knows no outcast humankind,
　　May serve and save the earth.

91

Whose purpose wealth can never turn,
　　Nor multitudes confound,
Though he may yet have much to learn,
　　His wisdom is profound.

92

The Empire's river, vast, divine,
  Is he in whose pure soul
Manhood and womanhood combine
  Into a childlike whole.

93

The Empire's model he shall be,
  Who knows both bad and good;
With him all virtue shall agree,
  All things be understood.

94

The Empire's valley is that one
  Who knows fame, but can see
His shame; and when his time is done
  Turns to simplicity.

95

The holy man who has recourse
  To this calm peace of mind,
Becomes a pure and powerful force
  To serve all humankind.

96

The Empire is divine; who take
    And mold it as they choose,
May mar, indeed, but never make;
    May take, but ever lose.

97

This has been said of humankind:
    "Some humble, others bold,
Some strong, some weak, cruel or kind,
    Some warm, and others cold."

98

Who may attempt to rule, and sway
    Into a common cause,
Save he who in the Godlike way
    Lets virtues be their laws?

99

War when you must, and only then,
    Nor put your faith in war;
War wastes the Empire's wealth of men,
    Then famine wastes far more.

100

Be resolute, but do not thrust
    Your weapon to its length;
Be resolute because you must,
    But not to prove your strength.

101

Things thrive and prosper and grow old
    And shortly pass away;
Thus end all things that do not hold
    To God and to His way.

102

In war, even the victors lose
    No less than the subdued;
So, the superior man will choose
    Content and quietude.

103

When he must fight, he will not fly;
    Winning, will not rejoice;
He does not love to see men die,
    And hear the widow's voice.

104

Who loves the battle, and to kill,
    And wastes the world with strife,
Shall not for long obtain his will,
    But surely lose his life.

105

As streams and creeks unite and flow
    In rivers to the sea,
God's mighty functions we may know
    Towards all things that be.

106

Unnamable, devoid of harm,
    Presuming not to press;
Yet, His simplicity and calm
    The world dare not suppress.

107

If kings and princes held Him fast
    Homage all things would pay,
The people would find peace at last,
    Disorder die away.

108

When out of God, good order came,
  After creation's storm;
The nameless had acquired a name,
  The namable, a form.

109

Dealing with forms, mankind may learn
  Just how far they may go,
And when to stop, and when to turn,
  Avoiding danger so.

110'

Who sums his fellows up at sight
  Brings wonder to their eyes;
But he who sums himself aright,
  Alone is truly wise.

111

Who would grind others into dust,
  Great power and strength will need;
But he who conquers his own lust
  Performs the greater deed.

112

What wealth is in a happy face!
    What vigor comes with will!
The enduring loses not his place;
    Dies, but continues still.

113

God's spirit is on every side,
    All things does He pervade;
In Him ten thousand things abide,
    By Him all things were made.

114

Nourishing all — below, above —
    He does not play the lord,
But spends Himself in perfect love,
    And asks for no reward.

115

The holy man who never needs
    The spurs of wealth and fame,
Shall leave a record of good deeds
    Greater than any name.

116

The whole wide world will come in quest
    Of him who holds this truth,
Which gives men peace and perfect rest
    And sempiternal youth.

117

When, from the wayside hotel, streams
    Music and savory scent,
The traveler stops; but wisdom seems
    Tasteless, and mute, and spent.

118

Who finds it, may not recognize,
    And so pass on his way;
But he whose heart is truly wise,
    Remains with it for aye.

119

Only the greater can grow less,
    Only the strong grow weak;
And he who falls to humbleness
    Once was not quite so meek.

120

He who is peaceful as a child
    And weak, need fear no wrong;
Thus is it that the meek and mild
    Conquer the hard and strong.

121

As fish, when drawn up from the sea
    Soon perish on the shore;
So should the people never be
    Seduced from peace to war.

122

If kings and princes exercised
    A non-assertive sway,
All evils soon would be revised,
    For that is God's good way.

123

In Godlike, calm simplicity
    Nothing remains undone,
And thus the people all might be
    To calm contentment won.

124

The fires of lust would leave their hearts
 And set their souls at rest;
Only when all desire departs
 May all the world be blest.

125

Inferior virtue never can
 Forego its virtuous claim;
Virtue, in the superior man,
 Knows nothing of the name.

126

Such virtue walks in God's own ways,
 Asserts not, nor pretends;
Not virtuous because it pays
 Or helps in making friends.

127

Benevolence is that good will
 Which works without reward;
How unlike justice — quick to kill,
 Dependent on the sword!

128

Propriety lays down its rules,
  And then has swift recourse
To justice and to sharp-edged tools,
  Its rulings to enforce.

129

Propriety is last of all;
  Next justice stands arrayed;
Good will succeeds to virtue's fall;
  And virtue is God's shade.

130

Tradition is of God the flower,
  But leads to ignorance;
For surely that shall lose its power,
  Whose power does not advance.

131

Therefore the holy man eschews
  The bud, the flower, the fruit;
External things he will refuse,
  Returning to the root.

132

In unity is greatest strength,
    It makes the heavens pure;
Through it, minds become souls at length;
    In it, earth shall endure.

133

Through unity, the valley gains
    Repletion for its fields,
And gathers to itself the rains
    To multiply its yields.

134

Through unity, ten thousand things
    Were called to life and breath;
Through unity, the ancient kings
    Controlled both life and death.

135

Without it, heaven might be rent;
    And earth might bend awry;
Minds unensouled be impotent;
    And valleys soon run dry.

136

Who will not take eternal life,
  How may he hope to live?
And what can kings expect but strife.
  Who ask more than they give?

137

The nobles and the kings depend
  Upon the commonweal;
For he who'd reach his journey's end
  Needs more than just one wheel.

138

Who knows his origin and stem
  In unity alone,
Will heed not praising as a gem
  Nor scorning as a stone.

139

In nothingness is God's great force,
  From that, existence came;
And thence, ere He turns to His source,
  All things with form and name.

140

Superior men who hear of it,
    Walk in the Godlike way;
And average men, of lesser wit,
    Strive, but oft disobey.

141

But when the inferior man, the fool,
    Takes the book in his hands,
He demonstrates by ridicule
    How much he understands.

142

It does not deal with lusts of earth
    Such as all fools perceive,
So only men of genuine worth,
    May know it and believe.

143

Therefore 'tis written that God's light
    Seems darkness twice distilled;
And he who leans upon His might,
    Seems weak and feeble-willed.

144

When he has done his simple best
    He asks for no reward,
But acts as humbly as a guest
    And does not play the lord.

145

His virtue is so circumspect
    Who puts in God his trust,
That lesser men can but suspect
    How he conceals their lust.

146

Who shows perfection to the less
    Can but expect their hate,
For, otherwise, they must confess
    Themselves not quite so great.

147

Yet only God's self can impart
    Completion to the soul,
And some day every human heart
    Shall comprehend the whole.

148

From God was the eternal name,
    And thence the Two had birth,
And then the Trinity, whence came
    All things in heaven and earth.

149

Sustained by earth, encompassed round
    By heaven serene and pure;
And yet it is the soundless sound
    That renders all secure.

150

Those who are truly fit to reign
    Are neither harsh nor proud;
For gain is loss, and loss is gain
    To one who wears a shroud.

151

How very ancient is this truth
    Which I propound once more!
And yet it has eternal youth
    Because it is the law.

152

The weakest thing in all the world
    Is water; yet its play,
Between the rocky ledges whirled,
    Grinds the hard rock away.

153

Water does not assert its might,
    But follows flow and fall;
Just so, who lives in wisdom's light
    Shall serve and conquer all.

154

Which is the nearer — self or name?
    Which dearer — self or gold?
And shall we count these things the same—
    That which we lose, and hold?

155

When aged people have great wealth,
    Either they squander all,
Or thieves and robbers come by stealth
    To break the treasure hall.

156

Who works not for a stated goal,
    Or to avoid a hell,
Shall lose his life and find his soul
    In joy of working well.

157

Perfection is not yet complete,
    Or all would cease to be;
Yet, even then, all would repeat
    Throughout eternity.

158

The straightest lines resemble curves;
    Great skill is never shown;
And he whom eloquence most serves,
    Never lets it be known.

159

Behold how motion conquers cold,
    And quietude conquers heat;
Just so the clear and pure behold
    All things beneath their feet.

160

When men accept God for their needs
    And each has all he asks,
Race horses, and more warlike steeds,
    Shall fall to menial tasks.

161

His sin is greatest who is rent
    By passion and desire;
The greatest woe is discontent,
    And greed the hottest fire.

162

Who takes contentment to his breast
    Shall find it pure and whole,
And know the bliss of perfect rest,
    In an enlightened soul.

163

In God, I may prognosticate
    The world and all its ways,
Yet never pass beyond my gate,
    Nor through my window gaze.

164

The further that the traveler goes
    In strange, exotic lands,
The less he sees, the less he knows,
    The less he understands.

165

And so the holy man remains,
    And does not travel far;
His wisdom, not for human brains,
    Embraces every star.

166

Because he knows the soul of things
    Their forms he need not meet.
He does not labor, yet he brings
    That which makes all complete.

167

Increase will follow learnedness,
    But, fed from heaven's store,
The holy man grows less and less,
    And so grows more and more.

168

Arrived at non-assertion's goal,
 The throne may be his ward;
For none is fit to rule the whole
 Who loves to play the lord.

169

The saint does more than stand aside
 From passion and from strife;
The circle of his heart is wide,
 Including all with life.

170

Those who are good he greets with good,
 And greets the bad the same;
For thus is goodness understood
 By those who know its name.

171

The faithful, and the faithless too,
 He meets with faith serene;
For that is how they always do,
 Who know what faith may mean.

172

The nobles treat him with respect,
　　He treats each like a child,
Anxious, indeed, and circumspect,
　　But tolerant and mild.

173

Thirteen roadways run through life
　　To thirteen doors of death;
Homeward, from foolish fears and strife,
　　We float on failing breath.

174

Why does man die? Because he lives
　　Intensely, with desire.
It is intensity that gives
　　His flesh to feed that fire.

175

I understand that one whose life
　　Is based on perfect good,
Shall walk in safety through fierce strife,
　　Or danger-haunted wood.

176

He does not fear the shining blade,
  Nor the fierce beast of prey;
Of mortal stuff he is not made,
  So none may touch or slay.

177

God quickens, and then virtues feed;
  Reality gives form;
And force completes; thus all things heed
  Virtue and virtue's norm.

178

None orders the ten thousand things
  To join in virtue's praise;
And so spontaneously it springs
  From love of virtue's ways.

179

To quicken things, but not to own;
  To make, but not to claim;
To raise, but not to seize the throne:
  That is eternal fame.

180

When the world turns to its youth,
　　Then God is recognized
As the world-mother, and this truth
　　Is understood and prized.

181

As one who knows his mother, so
　　In turn she knows her son;
She quickens him and helps him grow,
　　And guards till life is done.

182

Who sets aside desire, and rests
　　(Closing the gates of sense)
Calmly upon the mother's breasts,
　　Encounters no offense.

183

But he who gives himself to talk,
　　And meddles with affairs,
Throughout his life shall seem to walk
　　Down dim and dangerous stairs.

184

True wisdom brings humility;
   The tender are the strong:
Who practises these truths shall be
   Preserved from every wrong.

185

What little knowledge I possess
   Keeps me secure in grace;
In self-assertion growing less,
   Seeking not praise nor place.

186

How broad this mighty roadway seems!
   But people love the lanes
That lead them down beside the streams
   Of pleasures and of pains.

187

When palaces become immense,
   The fields are bare of sheaves.
To glory in the lusts of sense —
   This is the pride of thieves!

188

The tree no storm-wind can uproot
    Is planted in deep earth.
The treasure none can ever loot
    Is that of greatest worth.

189

His sons and grandsons shall not cease
    To hold his name in awe,
Who walks upon the way of peace,
    And keeps the perfect law.

190

Who walks alone in wisdom's beam,
    His virtue is not small.
But, ah, his virtue is supreme
    Who holds it out to all.

191

It is the way of man to test
    The unknown by the known;
By his own heart he weighs his guest,
    Ranks countries by his own.

192

He who has God within his heart
    Is like a little child:
Supremely strong in every part,
    Yet tender, soft, and mild.

193

The poisoned sting, the fang, the beak,
    Strike not, nor seize, nor tear;
His grasp, although his bones be weak,
    Is firm beyond compare.

194

He does not yield to passion's gusts,
    But keeps his person pure;
He loves indeed, but never lusts,
    And so he shall endure.

195

Who has this perfect harmony,
    Knows the eternal light;
But he who has it not, shall be
    Plunged in perpetual night.

196

They talk the most who know the least;
    One who is truly wise
Does not presume to play the priest,
    But shuts his mouth and eyes.

197

He is not moved by love or hate,
    By favor or disgrace;
To loss he is inviolate,
    And so he holds his place.

198

With rectitude one rules the states;
    With craftiness one leads
The army; but who serves and waits,
    Performs the greater deeds.

199

The more their rulers ring them round
    With rule and law and act,
The poorer are the people found
    In spirit and in fact.

200

States which are best prepared for war
    Are certain to conflict.
There is the least regard for law,
    Where laws are harsh and strict.

201

The holy man will never try
    To rule with sword or rod;
Content to set his standard high;
    He leaves the rest to God.

202

A prying government will do
    The people endless harm;
He is the wiser ruler, who
    Governs in peace and calm.

203

Misery rests on happiness,
    And under that again —
Although the foolish cannot guess —
    Lie misery and pain.

204

Thus everything in life depends
　　Upon its own reverse;
As enemies depend on friends,
　　And prose depends on verse.

205

And good on bad, as bad on good;
　　As courage rests on fear:
Only the rash and reckless could
　　Presume to interfere.

206

The holy man will never feel
　　Impatient to improve,
Because he knows the mighty wheel
　　Must turn in its own groove.

207

To govern men is God's affair;
　　And what presumptuous clod,
In awful arrogance, shall dare
　　To take the place of God?

208

Indeed he has a mighty task
 Who governs his own soul,
And shall such imperfection ask
 The right to rule the whole?

209

Practising virtue, truth, and thrift,
 Himself, and every day;
Thus only may he hope to lift
 Another on the way.

210

Those rulers who sincerely wish
 Their service not to fail,
Will govern as one fries small fish,
 And neither gut nor scale.

211

Who governs in the holy name,
 And not with idle talk,
Shall keep the country's demons tame,
 Nor shall its specters walk.

212

And neither shall the sages, then,
 Incite rebelliousness;
But demons, ghosts, and holy men
 Shall join to serve and bless.

213

A great state, one that lowly flows,
 Becomes the empire's wife;
Because, through quietude, she knows
 And rules her husband's life.

214

Through lowliness towards small states,
 The great state conquers all;
Just as great ones, forcing their fates,
 Are conquered by the small.

215

So some adopt their lowliness
 Because they wish the name;
Others are lowly by duress,
 But conquer just the same.

216

A great state should desire no more
    Than to unite and feed.
A smaller state, avoiding war,
    Must serve the people's need.

217

But so that both may do their tasks,
    The greater one must bend;
Not proudly, but as one who asks
    The right to serve a friend.

218

The universe finds joy and health
    In him who walks God's way;
He is the good man's greatest wealth,
    The bad man's surest stay.

219

With cunning words, a man may sell
    That which is poor or bad;
Had he been honest, who can tell
    What gain he might have had?

220

If any man be found with sin,
    Shall he be held as naught?
And yet that is the custom in
    The Emperor's own court.

221

Better than justice, swift to kill,
    And urging men to strife,
It is to do the Father's will,
    And speak the word of life.

222

Why did the ancients prize that word?
    Because, when sinners craved
To hear it, it was always heard,
    And so were sinners saved.

223

Asserting self invites a fall;
    Keep yourself safe from such;
Learning to magnify the small,
    And make the little much.

224

With perfect love and virtue, woo
    The one who proffers hate.
Learn to begin what you must do
    Before it grows too great.

225

Remember that the greatest task,
    That conquers human will,
Was tiny once, and did not ask
    Vast wisdom or much skill.

226

The wise man will not play the great,
    Thus greatness will achieve;
For self-assurance tempts ill fate,
    And braggarts none believe.

227

Regarding nothing as too light
    To need his utmost skill,
All difficulties fade from sight,
    And he attains his will.

228

Things still at rest need not be feared,
    They may be kept content;
And that which has not yet appeared,
    'Tis easy to prevent.

229

What is still feeble may be burst
    Asunder with a touch;
What is still scant may be dispersed
    Before it grows too much.

230

Anticipate the thing to be,
    And so prevent the deed.
Remember that the stoutest tree
    Came from a tiny seed.

231

With brick on bricks, and tile on tiles,
    One builds a massive wall.
The journey of a thousand miles
    Begins with one footfall.

232

What common people undertake
    Tires them e'er they begin.
They only mar what they would make,
    And lose what they would win.

233

Who does not guard his enterprise
    Until he gains his goal,
Often is taken by surprise
    That robs him of the whole.

234

The wise man limits his desires,
    And does not mount too high;
But kindles his domestic fires
    Where multitudes pass by.

235

He helps indeed, with mind and hands,
    When nature's will is clear;
But otherwise he understands
    And does not interfere.

236

The ancient ones who ruled of yore,
    And knew whereof they spoke,
Said: "Do not cast the sacred lore
    Among the common folk.

237

"Much knowledge will corrupt the heart,
    When partly understood,
And so the people grow too smart,
    But neither wise nor good.

238

"Ruling with smartness is a curse,
    He who would serve and bless
His country's people, might do worse
    Than just to rule them less."

239

Who rules according to this plan
    Has virtue most profound;
Modeling on the holy man,
    He too, shall be renowned.

240

Through valleys deep, great rivers flow
　　To swell the deeper sea;
And it, because it lies so low,
　　Greatest of all may be.

241

And so the holy man who seeks
　　To serve his people's needs
Must keep beneath them when he speaks,
　　Behind them when he leads.

242

Because he seems no more than they,
　　The people will not hate,
But mark his wisdom and obey
　　And strive to emulate.

243

Striving with no one, no one can
　　Confront him with the sword.
The world will always praise that man
　　Who asks for no reward.

244

A man must differ to be great;
  What greatness is expressed
By him who shares the common fate,
  And follows all the rest?

245

I have three treasures which I prize:
  Compassion first, then thrift,
And third, not daring to arise
  However much I lift.

246

Who has compassion can be brave,
  And who has thrift can give;
The life one does not seek to save,
  Enables one to live.

247

Those who are brave but never kind,
  Generous but always poor,
Ambitious, not of modest mind:
  These shall not long endure.

248

Compassion is victorious
    When driven to attack;
And in defense 'tis glorious
    Even when driven back.

249

The greatest warriors often hate
    The very thought of strife.
Who takes up weapons to be great,
    Shall surely lose his life.

250

He shall excel who never strives,
    Who strives shall not excel.
He who would govern others' lives
    Must govern his own well.

251

And that employer is most wise
    Who follows heaven's plan,
In learning how to utilize
    The worth of every man.

252

A famous general once observed:
    "Act not the host in war,
But act the guest, and be reserved;
    Accomplish, then withdraw."

253

Who dares to hold his foemen light,
    Commits the worst of sins;
For when matched armies meet and fight,
    Compassion always wins.

254

How easy are these words I speak,
    How simple to achieve!
Yet, through the world, in vain I seek
    For one who can believe.

255

That which is more than deed and word,
    No one can comprehend;
What wonder that I am not heard,
    Or, being heard, offend!

256

Therefore the holy man confides
    But little in his kind;
Dresses in wool, and deeply hides
    His jewels in his mind.

257

To know that which is never shown,
    Is spiritual wealth;
But not to know what may be known,
    Is madness and ill health.

258

Yet only those who know their need
    Are anxious to be pure;
And so ill health will often lead
    The sinner to the cure.

259

When people lose the sense of fear,
    The dreadful shall befall;
But life is neither sad nor drear
    To one who lives it all.

260

The wise man will observe his heart,
    And yield not to displays;
Endeavoring to play his part,
    He will not seek for praise.

261

Daring is deadly; courage leads
    To life, serene and calm;
Yet both of these contain the seeds
    Of benefit and harm.

262

The heavenly reason never strives,
    Yet is its purpose pure.
Though it speaks not, nor seems alive,
    Its victory is sure.

263

The net of heaven is vast, so vast;
    Its meshes wide, so wide;
And yet it gathers all things fast,
    And none is left outside.

264

If folk were not afraid to die,
    What mandarin or lord
Could hope to subjugate them by
    Threats of the blade and cord?

265

If, knowing death's illusion well,
    We let folks fear it still;
And, notwithstanding, some rebel,
    Shall we, too, dare to kill?

266

When human beings arrogate
    The right to judge and slay,
They but usurp the power of fate
    Which none but God may sway.

267

So tightly binds the mystic mesh
    That winds about the whole;
The sword that wounds another's flesh,
    Pierces his judge's soul.

268

The people hunger when the lords
        Demand too great a tax;
And they rebel when bars and cords
        Are brothers to the axe.

269

Be not so strict in ruling life;
        Let God pursue His course.
For striving leads only to strife,
        And force arouses force.

270

Man during life is tender, warm;
        But dead is stiff and cold.
So is it, too, with every form
        That all the kingdoms hold.

271

Thus the hard, the strong, the great,
        Are like to things of death;
The tender and the delicate
        Are brothers of the breath.

272

The greater human greatness grows,
    The greater is its fall.
The truly great remain below;
    The tender conquer all.

273

As one who stretches on a bow,
    So are the heavenly fates;
The proud and lofty they bring low,
    The low they elevate.

274

From those who have too much, they take
    Wherewith to help along
Those who have little. But men make
    The weak support the strong.

275

Yet wealth is only good to spend,
    And strength to help the weak.
He shall be greatest in the end
    Who served but did not seek.

276

How delicate the flowing stream,
　　And yet it wears away
The rugged rock, the hardened beam,
　　With little more than spray.

277

And so in life, the weak are those
　　Who win the greater prize:
A truth that everybody knows,
　　Yet no one ever tries.

278

Who makes his country's sin his own,
　　We hail as our high priest;
And who will for her curse atone,
　　We crown him at the feast.

279

The wise man, dealing with mankind,
　　Gives more than his full tale;
But wipes the matter from his mind,
　　If others chance to fail.

280

He knows that broken faith may lead
    To hatred and sharp blame,
Which, when the wounds have ceased to
                            bleed,
    Leaves things not quite the same.

281

And so the holy man attends
    His duty, not his due;
And him the heavens will befriend
    In all that he may do.

282

In a small country with few folk
    Let rulers hide their power;
Let people grieve at death, not joke,
    Nor try to flee the hour.

283

Though they have carriages and boats,
    They shall not ride away.
Though they have swords and armored
                            coats,
    They shall not fight nor slay.

284

So was it in the ancient days,
    So let it be once more.
Let us return to simple ways,
    Forgetting greed and war.

285

Let man find pleasure in his food,
    And comfort in his home;
Knowing his country to be good,
    He shall not wish to roam.

286

True words often are hard to bear,
    And pleasant words untrue;
And so the sage will never dare
    To force his teachings through.

287

And yet he will not hoard them, for
    None knows as well as he,
The more he gives away, the more
    His own supply shall be.

288

He will not argue, then, nor strive,
    And yet will never cease
His toil, till everyone alive
    Has seen and known GOD'S PEACE.

This book is one of the Quest Miniature Series, a special imprint of the Theosophical Publishing House. Other Quest Miniatures are:

At the Feet of the Master *by Alcyone*
The Buddhist Catechism *by Henry Steel Olcott*
Circle of Wisdom *by Helena Petrovna Blavatsky*
An Experience of Enlightenment *by Flora Courtois*
Finding Deep Joy *by Robert Ellwood*
Finding the Quiet Mind *by Robert Ellwood*
Fragments *by C. Jinarajadasa*
Freedom Through the Balisier *by Cyril H. Boynes*
From the Outer Court to the Inner Sanctum
by Annie Besant
Gifts of the Lotus *Comp. by Virginia Hanson*
Hymn of Jesus *by G. R. S. Mead*
Light on the Path *by Mabel Collins*
Natural Man *by Henry David Thoreau*
Reflective Meditation *by Kay Mouradian*
The Sage From Concord
Comp. by V. Hanson and C. Pedersen
The Song Celestial *by Sir Edwin Arnold*
Tao *by Charles H. Mackintosh*
Thoughts for Aspirants *by N. Sri Ram*
Trust Yourself to Life *by Clara Codd*
Voice of the Silence *by Helena Petrovna Blavatsky*

Available from:
QUEST BOOKS
306 West Geneva Road
Wheaton, Illinois 60187